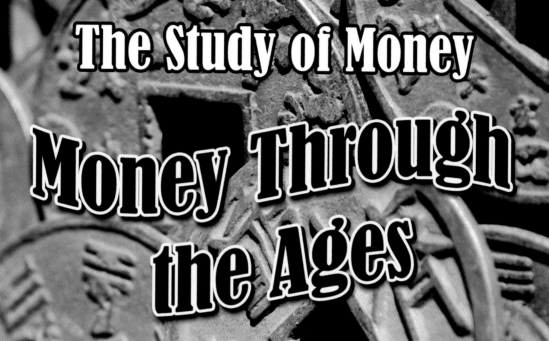

The Study of Money

Money Through the Ages

Tim Clifford

Rourke
Publishing LLC
Vero Beach, Florida 32964

www.rourkepublishing.com

PHOTO CREDITS:© Feng Yu: Title Page; © STILLFX: page 4 top; © PhotoDisc: page 4 middle: © Pavlova Elena: page 4 bottom; © Kelly Cline: page 5; © Lisa F. Young: page 6; © Bryan Busovicki: page 7; © LinaArt: page 8; © narvikk: page 9 top; © Eric Isselée: page 9 bottom; © BrickTop: page 10; © Shi Yali, © Scott Rothstein, © C.T. Snow: page 11; © Donald R. Swartz: page 13 top; © Jo Ann Snover: page 13 bottom; © Kenneth V. Pilon: page 14 top; © Keith Wheatley: page 14 bottom left; © jam4travel: page 14 bottom right; © PHG, © 300dpi: page 15; © Mike McDonald: page 17 top; US Treasury: page 17 bottom, 19; © Vincent Giordano: page 18; © John S. Sfondilias: page 19 bottom; © Sam DCruz: page 20; © Mikael Damkier: page 21; Library of Congress: page 22 top; © Gregory James Van Raalte: page 24; © Gina Sanders: page 25; ©Huang Yuetao: page 26; © Marco Arments: page 27 top; © forzaq: page 27 bottom; © Darren Green: page 28; © Jaimie Duplass: page 29; © Lev Olkha: page 30

Editor: Jeanne Sturm

Cover Design: Renee Brady

Page Design: Tara Raymo

Library of Congress Cataloging-in-Publication Data

Clifford, Tim, 1959-
 Money through the ages / Tim Clifford.
    p. cm. -- (The study of money)
 Includes index.
 ISBN 978-1-60472-406-6
 1. Money--Juvenile literature. I. Title.
 HG221.5.C57 2009
 332.4'9--dc22

                                         2008011333

Printed in the USA

IG/IG

Table of Contents

What is Money?

When you think of money, you may think of bills or coins. Have you ever thought of a cow as a type of money? How about a seashell? Money has taken many forms over the centuries, but whether it's a cow or a coin, money serves a purpose.

Money can be exchanged for goods or services, or used to pay a **debt**. Long before the invention of the printing press and paper money, people used many different methods of paying for what they needed.

Imagine a world without money. If you were a corn farmer, you'd have to find someone who needed corn in order to buy anything. Even worse, after the corn season was over, you'd have nothing to pay with at all.

In a world with money, however, you would be able to exchange your corn for money. Then, you'd be able to buy anything you needed at any time of year.

Bartering

Have you ever traded baseball cards or marbles with your friends? If you have, you were bartering. Before early forms of money were developed, everyone used to **barter**. This simple form of exchanging goods probably existed before recorded history.

Long ago, almost all people were farmers, so bartering made a lot of sense. People could trade the livestock or the crops they grew for other types of food.

While bartering worked for the most part, it did have some drawbacks. The biggest one was that you needed to find someone to barter with. If that trading partner didn't want what you had to offer, you couldn't do business.

Bartering is as old as recorded history. Yet, it is still used today. People and governments barter all sorts of goods and services.

7

Early Forms of Money

Bartering worked because animals of a certain size, or a certain amount of wheat, had similar values. That meant they could be exchanged for items of equal value.

Of course, it wasn't always convenient to drag a cow or a bushel of corn around in order to buy things. People needed to find something they could easily use to pay for goods. Many things were tried over the centuries, such as beads and even dog teeth!

Whatever ancient people used as money, it had to be easy to carry around. People tried using food as money, such as rice, but food goes bad. It was clear that money needed to be **durable**, or strong enough to last a long time.

In addition, to be of value, money needed to be accepted by others. It also needed to have a certain value that could easily be traded.

9

Funny Money

There have been many unusual forms of money throughout history. One of the earliest was the cowry. The **cowry** is the shell of a sea snail. The shell is shiny and smooth, and can vary in size from small to large.

Cowries were used by civilizations around the world. Their colorful design and durability made them popular as money in Africa, China, India, and North America.

Other Funny Money

Here are some other unusual forms of money used throughout the ages.

 Early Romans used salt as money. Chunks of salt of a certain size could be traded.

 Ancient Egyptians used gold and silver rings to pay for goods. This type of money was very easy to carry.

 Tribes in the Celtic regions of Europe also used rings and jewelry as money.

 Yap islanders of the Pacific used donut shaped stones as money. Some stones were as large as 12 feet across.

Gold and Silver Coins

The first coins were minted around 600 B.C. in ancient Lydia. These coins were made of electrum, which is an **alloy** of gold and silver. Because each coin contained about the same amount of precious metals, they could be exchanged easily as money.

The remains of ancient shops were found at the archaeological site of Sardis, in Turkey.

These first coins were stamped with a lion's head. By striking them with a hammer on an anvil, a picture could be produced. Today's technology uses high speed minting presses.

Gold and silver coins have remained popular over the centuries because of the value of their metal. Most governments have stopped making these coins because the gold and silver is worth more than the **face value** of the coin. The face value is the amount stamped on the coin.

Did you know...

Did you know that there is a coin with no face value stamped on it? It is the South African Krugerrand. This coin contains one troy ounce of gold, so it is worth whatever an ounce of gold is worth. The first Krugerrands were minted in 1967. Because the price of gold has gone up since then, so has the value of the coin.

Ancient Coins

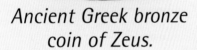

Ancient Greek bronze coin of Zeus.

The ancient Greeks were the first to look at coins as a form of art. They loved making beautiful coins engraved with pictures of Greek gods.

Important people were also celebrated on coins. The ancient Romans stamped images of their emperors on coins. This tradition continues today. We honor presidents, such as George Washington, on our money. Important historical figures, such as Benjamin Franklin, also appear on American money.

Roman silver coin showing Emperor Philip I.

American coin showing George Washington.

Coins became an important part of money systems all over the world. Ancient coins came in a wide variety of shapes and styles.

Coins of the Ancient World

India		Many coins from India were of an irregular shape. Punches on the front showed where and when a coin was made.
China		An unusual feature of these coins is the square hole in the center.
England		The English stamped portraits of their kings on coins.
United States		The Chain Cent was the first coin minted in the USA, in 1793.

15

Representative Money

With gold and silver coins, the value was in the coins themselves. In many countries, a system of **representative money** developed. In this system, the money itself was worth nothing—it was made of paper or cheap metals, such as copper. The government, however, would make a promise to back up the money or exchange it for silver or gold.

In the United States, representative money was used from the late 19th to the early 20th century.

Will Pay to the Bearer on Demand

Gold and Silver Certificates

For a time, you could take U.S. paper money to the bank and exchange it for silver or gold! These **certificates** were official **currency** in the United States.

Silver Certificate

Gold Certificate

Back of Gold Certificate

17

Fiat Money

How much gold will the government give you for a dollar today? The answer may surprise you: none. Most of the money in the world today is **fiat money**, or money that is not backed by gold or other metals.

The word fiat comes from the Latin for *let it be done*. In other words, fiat money is accepted because a government declares it official money. Unlike gold coins, fiat money itself is worth nothing.

Governments often use fiat money systems because they need more money than they have.

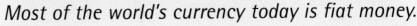

Most of the world's currency today is fiat money.

The United States has switched back and forth between fiat money and gold- or silver-backed money. The use of fiat money can often be traced to historical events when the government needed money.

1775—To pay for the Revolutionary War, the United States issued Continentals, the first fiat money.

1862—To pay for the Civil War, the United States issued fiat currency called Greenbacks. These notes were green on the reverse side.

19

History of Banks

As long as money has been around, people have needed banks to keep it safe. The earliest banks were ancient religious temples where people stored the grain or precious metals they used as money.

Like today's banks, these temples were well built. That helped keep money safe. Because banks were also religious places, it was unlikely that anyone would steal from them. Over time, ancient banks began to loan money to people who needed it.

The first banks existed thousands of years ago. Although they look very different today, banks perform many of the same functions they did in ancient times. They still store and loan money. In addition, modern banks issue checks, credit cards, and money orders.

ATMs, or Automated Teller Machines, have changed how people use banks. You can deposit or withdraw money wherever there is an ATM machine. In cities, there may be an ATM on every corner!

North American Money

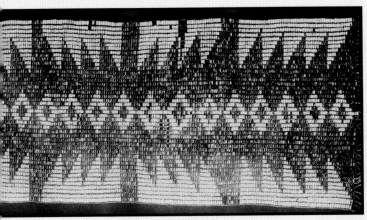

Wampum

Early Native Americans traded wampum. These strings of white whelk shells were used as money. American settlers began to use wampum as well.

The Spanish dollar was accepted as money in the United States until 1857. Widely known as *pieces of eight*, these dollars could be used whole or cut into halves, quarters, and eighths.

Spanish Pieces of Eight Dollar

This currency is still used today in the United States and Canada.

People accepted the Spanish dollar throughout North America. These were the first dollars used in America and Canada. Later on, both the United States and Canada began printing their own dollars.

Mexico began using the peso, which is very similar in size and weight to the Spanish dollar.

Peso

Spanish Dollar

Money around the World

There is an amazing variety of money used throughout the world today. It comes in many shapes, sizes, and colors. China uses the yuan, Japan uses the yen, and India uses the rupee.

In recent centuries, most countries have issued their own money. That is now beginning to change with the introduction of the euro.

The Chinese Yuan

The Japanese Yen

The Indian Rupee

For a long time, the United States dollar was the most popular currency in the world. Ever since its introduction in 1999, the euro started catching up.

The euro is the official currency of the European Union. Fifteen countries now use it. They include Austria, Belgium, Cyprus, Finland, France, Germany, Greece, Ireland, Italy, Luxembourg, Malta, the Netherlands, Portugal, Slovenia, and Spain.

Exchanging Currency

In the ancient past, people rarely traveled beyond their own countries, so they only needed one form of currency. Today, things are different. If you fly to England, which uses the British pound, your dollars won't be accepted. You must use the currency of the country you visit.

To do this, you must exchange your money for the currency of that country. This can be confusing, because one United States dollar is not equal to one British pound, or one Chinese yuan, or any other currency.

26

To make things worse, the value of a currency can go up or down every day! A **currency exchange** can help you trade in your money for the right amount of foreign currency.

EXCHANGE RATES

	"TRANSFER"		"CASH"
	WE SELL AT	WE BUY AT	WE SELL AT
US DOLLAR	0.28869	0.29069	0.291.19
JAPANESE YEN	0.00240	0.00242	
SWISS FRANC	0.23822	0.24001	0.24047
BRITISH POUND	0.57599	0.58033	0.58133
EURO EUR	0.39392	0.39693	0.39671
CANADIAN DOLLAR	0.25841	0.26041	0.26086
DANISH KRONE			
EGYPTION POUND	0.50671	5.12202	
BAHRANI DINAR	7.63246	7.70917	7.70917
QATARI RIYAL	0.07901	0.07981	0.07981
SAUDI RIYAL	0.07693	0.07749	0.07765
U.A.E. DIRHAM	0.78340	0.07912	0.07912
INDIAN RUPEE	0.00693	0.00699	
PAK. RUPEE	0.00475	0.00479	
ITALIAN LIRA	0.00604	0.00610	
FRENCH FRANC	0.00262	0.00264	
DEUTSCHE MARK	0.00415	0.00421	
SPANISH PESETA	0.23814	0.24002	

An exchange rate display shows how much one currency is worth in comparison to another.

Electronic Money

Money has changed a great deal over the years. Electronic money may be the most revolutionary change of all. Instead of carrying your money in your pockets, you can send money all over the world instantly via computer.

Using the Internet, many electronic money systems simply **transfer** money from one bank account to another.

Today we can transfer money electronically from an ATM or a home computer.

With electronic money, you can use your computer to pay for goods and services. You can purchase items, participate in auctions, or pay bills all without using a single coin or piece of paper money.

The Future of Money

We have come a long way since the days when large stones were used as money. Many things are bought and sold without the use of physical money at all.

The form of money changes all the time. From dog teeth to gold coins to paper money to electronic payments, money has been part of society for many generations. While it is impossible to say what form money will take next, it is certain that money will remain an important part of our lives and cultures.

30

Glossary

alloy (AL-oi): a mixture of two or more metals

barter (BAR-tur): to trade by exchanging food or other goods or services

certificates (sur-TIF-uh-kits): documents that show ownership

cowry (KOU-ree): the shell of a sea snail

currency (KUR-uhn-see): the form of money used in a country

debt (det): an amount of money that you owe

durable (DUR-uh-buhl): tough and lasting for a long time

face value (FAYSS VAL-yoo): the amount stamped on a coin or printed on paper money

fiat money (FEE-aht MUHN-ee): money that is not backed by gold or other metals

precious (PRESH-uhss): rare and valuable

representative money (rep-ri-ZEN-tuh-tiv MUHN-ee): money made of paper or cheap metals that a government promises to back up or exchange for silver or gold

transfer (TRANSS-fur): to move money from one account to another

Index

Further Reading

Eagleton, Catherine, et al. *Money: A History*. Firefly Books, 2007.
Godfrey, Neale S. *Ultimate Kid's Money Book*. Aladdin, 2002.

Websites

http://www.historyforkids.org/learn/economy/money.htm
http://library.thinkquest.org/C004203/economic/economic01.htm
http://www.pbs.org/wgbh/nova/moolah/history.html

About the Author

Tim Clifford is an educational writer and the author of many nonfiction children's books. He has two wonderful daughters and two energetic Border Collies that he adopted from a shelter. Tim became a vegetarian because of his love for animals. He is also a computer nut and a sports fanatic. He lives and works in New York City as a public school teacher.